Sleeping Sound &

Single

A Woman's Guide to Understanding God's Love, Developing Self Love and Finding the Love of Your Life

SHENIQUE GREENE

Printed in the United States of America

www.SheniqueGreene.com

@SheniqueG on Instagram

First Printing, 2017

ISBN 978-0-692-79960-4

Book Cover Design by Books Design by Ana Grigoriu-Voicu

Editing by Val Pugh-Love

This book is dedicated to
my Lord and Savior Jesus Christ
my mother, Yvonne
my grandmother, Thelma
my sisters, Sacha & Serena
my brothers, Brandon & Maurice
my best friend, love & soon to be husband, Mario

Thank you for always believing in me.

Most people are not running to the pleasure of being married but running from the pain of loneliness...

Contents

Introduction

Love is such a wonderful and beautiful thing. Most women love the idea of being loved and being in love. Many of us look forward to the day that we walk down the aisle in a beautiful white dress right into the arms of our knight in shining armor. We have been prepped to become a wife since we played with dolls as little girls. The funny thing is there is a big difference between our expectations and our reality as we become adults. So many times, we think that finding love is this major obstacle course that we must go through in life. Well, this is false! However, I can understand why you believe so...

You haven't found him, so either you're accepting mess from the men you're dating, or you've completely given up on finding someone. Sometimes the idea of that fairytale is exactly what keeps us from being able to recognize and find love. Society has created a false expectation of what love and relationships really are. Because of this, love can be looking us right in the face, yet we wouldn't know it. Just because it isn't what we think it should "look" like, we delay the possibility of it happening in our lives. We see love as a Cloud Nine, always perfect, instant connection. However, real love is nothing like that. In fact, it often comes unexpectedly and looks nothing like we imagined. But, since society has painted a false picture of love, we look for reality in superficial things. Then, the moment you meet someone who isn't your "type," you ignore the possibility of happily ever after.

As we go through life, we experience a lot of joy and pain, but there are many times when we take ownership of things (situations, relationships, etc.) that God never intended for us to ever deal with in the first place. Consequently, these experiences prevent us from having the things that God did intend for us to take possession of such as love, prosperity, joy, etc. In Genesis 2:18, the bible says, "It is not good that man should be alone. I will make him a helper…" the woman. So, there you have it. The woman was created to help the man fulfill the purpose that God planned for his life. This means you can't give up on love just because some relationships or things of the past didn't work out as you hoped or planned. It is God's plan for a man and woman to be in relationship with one another.

But, I get it! You've been dating for a while now, and boy has it been a struggle! You are frustrated because you haven't quite found *the one.* You've dealt with heartbreaks, and you've become discouraged about finding love. You often ask yourself, "Will the day ever come?" I completely understand! I have been there; we all have. However, it's time for us to move on from the hurt, learn from our mistakes, correct them, and adjust accordingly. God's word says, "Therefore a man shall leave his father and his mother and hold fast to his wife, and they shall become one flesh." So, guess what, girlie? God's intention is for a man and woman to become one, and it's time for us women to start acting like it.

I know that we all just want to be loved and have that special man to love us back. Please understand that this book is a testimony, and it's proof that when you focus on God, He will give you all the desires of your heart. Let me tell you, I know your struggle! This past year, the Holy Spirit ministered to me about mistakes that we, as women, make in our relationships. When I say *we*, that also includes *me*! God had me to hold the mirror up so that I could see what I was doing wrong. Then, He told me how to correct it and that I had share it with you. He loves you so much that He got me right so that I could help you become who He desires for us to be. It is no coincidence that you picked this book up, but you must be willing to make some changes to become a better you.

Women have so much power, and it's time we recognize it. It's time we make better choices with who we choose to date, procreate with, and become one with. Yes, the man is the head of the household, but WE choose the man so that he can be in that position. We must be able to select men who can meet our requirements and stop settling for just anyone to fill the void. An accounting firm does not hire a CPA who has never taken an Accounting class. That class is a prerequisite to ensure that the CPA has learned the right stuff before coming onboard with the firm. The same should be expected in relationships. Why are we allowing men who don't qualify for the position to fill the job? We don't have to settle, and it's time we start acting like we know this. Consider this an accountability call! It's time to wake up, ladies.

I have included my personal life examples of how I learned from my mistakes and became a better woman. The number one question I get is what exactly did I do? I simply got closer to God through His word. As you continue to read this book, pay attention to the scriptures that I have included at the end of each chapter to help with each topic. I suggest you spend time with these scriptures and meditate on them. I have also included an area for you write notes and personal affirmations. If you have a hard time understanding the King James Version (KJV) of the Bible, I suggest that you invest in a New International Version (NIV) Study Bible. It has helped me tremendously in understanding the word. You can also download the Bible app on your cell phone and consider The Message version.

Chapter 1
Seek God

I want to start by asking a simple question... How is your relationship with God? Do you speak to Him daily? Do you ask Him for direction on your day to day tasks? I'm not talking about some bogus religious process that you have been taught throughout your life. I'm not referring to just going to church on Sunday, praying, shouting, and then not thinking about Him until the next Sunday. So, I'll ask you again... How is your RELATIONSHIP with Him? Do you talk to Him? Do you spend time with Him? Do you apply His word to how you are living your life? Do you praise Him?

Now, by no means do I mean to jump down your throat, but these are all vital questions. These questions will determine how close you are to the Most High. When you develop a relationship with the Father, you give Him the opportunity to speak to your heart and mind about the things that are necessary for your prosperity. Keep in mind that when I say *prosperity*, I don't mean just money, possessions, and accolades. I mean wholeness in every area of your life. I'm talking about mental, physical, emotional, and spiritual wholeness - nothing missing, nothing broken.

When we seek God, we give Him the authority to direct our paths and order our steps. Most of the time, we like to play God in our own lives. We completely leave Him out of our decisions until everything begins to fall apart. We create our own rules, and we just do what we want. You know, whatever feels good. Well guess what... Feelings change every single day, and for some of us, every hour. We have to get to a place where we seek Him in all that we do. It's funny because now that I think back on those days when I would only speak to Him on Sunday, I wonder how I got this far.

Finally, I just got tired of doing it my way. After so many failed attempts, I realized that it wasn't working. I was miserable, and I had no peace in my life. I just got to a place where I wanted Him to be the first thing I thought of in the morning and the last thing I thought of at night. Once I made that decision, my life changed. I began to spend more time in His word. I would talk to Him more throughout the day. I even stuck post-its and notes everywhere to remind myself of who I was in Him. I remember feeling so foolish because this was probably the millionth time that I was going to do right by God. How many of us have been there? When was the last time you said, "He ain't done with me yet!"?

Well, I was tired of straddling the fence. My finances were a mess. My romantic "relationship" was non-existent. I hated my job.

I was just in a place in life where I was lost. Things looked good on the outside, but on the inside, they weren't, and only I knew it. Thank God that He loved me enough to take me out of that dark place and show me the light. Have you ever been in this place or are you here now? I'm here to tell you that it's time to come out. It's time for you to understand your position of who you are in God, and allow Him to have access to your life. It's often hard for us to do this. We have this idea that God is this unreachable God who lives in the clouds. But, sis, I have good news. He is inside of you! All you need to do is open your mouth and ask Him to guide you. Once you do that, He will begin to work in you.

Another way I like to interact with God is by treating Him how I treat my mother. She appreciates when I call her… This is how you acknowledge Him. She appreciates when I talk to her… This is prayer. She appreciates when I spend time with her... This is reading His word. She appreciates when I thank her for being there for me... This is praise and worship. When I talk to her and she tells me she's going to do something, I hold her to that because that's her word and I believe what she says. I trust her. When I do these things with my mother, I begin to believe her more because of the strength of our bond. All these things are how I create and develop a relationship with my mom, and it's the exact same thing God wants from you. He wants to spend time and develop a relationship with you. He wants you to trust Him. He wants you to believe what He says. He wants you to know His word.

When I began to look at God as a parent, I started to see Him as a loving God. Before, I only saw Him as a punishing God. The truth is that He is your heavenly father, and He wants you to live a life of heaven on earth. He wants the best for you. He wants you to have the greatest relationships and continuous joy. He wants you to have peace, prosperity, and healing. After I got to know God as a parent, I learned that there was no way that the same God that I now trusted and believed would want me living a life of hurt, fear, or sadness. However, these were all the things that I was experiencing. I then realized that it was time for me to seek Him more intimately and allow Him to guide me.

I remember falling on my knees to pray to Him. It was such a simple prayer. I began to talk to Him like I talked to my best friend. "Help me God. This is not the life of a child of God. Give me direction on the things that you should have me to do." How many of us think that we should have this elaborate prayer for God to show up? Well, you don't. He is such a gracious, polite gentleman. He's just sitting there waiting for you to let Him work. If you don't take heed to anything else in this book, I encourage you to talk to God. Don't listen to what religion says about Him. All He wants you to do is believe, and He will do the rest.

Around the time that I said this prayer, my pastor was preaching about making confessions. He said that God was waiting for us to give heaven permission to go forth and work on our behalf. He advised that we should find the scriptures relating to what we were asking God for and remind God of what His word says. I didn't know what I was doing, but I trusted God and I knew that His word did not come back void. Therefore, I was obedient and wrote down everything that I was praying for, and I found a scripture that backed it up. I prayed about my car, my health, my finances, my self-esteem, my past, my relationship, my faith, my trust... Everything! Did you know that that bible has a scripture on every topic that you experience in life? This was in June of 2013. I began to confess the things that I wanted and what God promised for my life every single day. I gave everything to God. Would you believe that today, most of those things have manifested in my life? All I had to do was simply believe.

I must be honest with you. It sounds easy, but when I started to say these confessions, I felt insane. How could I believe that I was rich, when my bank account said otherwise? How could I call the guy I wanted to be with my husband, when he didn't even want to be in a relationship? How could I be confident when I felt unattractive and self-conscious about my body? I made the decision that God's promises were bigger than my senses. It didn't matter what it looked like or what I felt like. It didn't matter what the world said. I wasn't going to allow my feelings to get in the way of God's promises any longer. It was time to seek God and let Him have his way with my life.

Is it time for you to allow God to have His way with your life? Are you tired of doing things your way and getting the same results? I wonder how many times we have to have our hearts broken or have our bank accounts at zero before we stop relying on ourselves. It's time that we became rooted and grounded in His word so that we're not begging and pleading for Him to save us in the midnight hour.

Now, don't get me wrong... Yes, God shows up in the midnight hour. But, isn't it time for you to have so much trust in Him that you never even have a care or a worry? Aren't you tired of sweating bullets until that last second that He saves you? It's time to trust Him! I bet if you had a glimpse of the life that God has for you, you would quickly put Him first! His plans for us are bigger and greater than we could ask or imagine. His dreams for us are nothing that our natural mind can even fathom. Whoa! I bet that husband is in there, too! It's time to get our minds right daily. It's time to renew our minds with His word and change the way we think so that His thoughts become ours. Rejoice in the Lord, and He WILL give you the desires of your heart.

Well, as you all know, this is a relationship book. So, let's get to the nitty gritty. What I didn't realize is that when I gave everything to God, not only was He going to answer my prayers, but He was also going to deal with my issues. I wasn't even ready for what was about to happen in my life. The things that He exposed to me allowed me to deal with how I was blocking my blessing. I realized that I was the reason some things were going wrong in my life.

Are you standing in your own way? Are you stopping your happily ever after? When you begin to get closer to God there are going to be some things that may make you uncomfortable, but I promise that it will be worth it in the end. Just because you are used to doing something that does not mean it is right. Drama is not normal; however, some of us have become so accustomed to it that we accept it. As you grow and change, it will hurt and it will be a little rough, but you can do it. God wants the best for you, but you will never receive what He has for you with your old way of thinking and doing things. It is time that you renew your mind with His word.

Scriptures on Seeking God

- ♥ Deuteronomy 4:29 – "But from there you will seek the Lord your God and you will find him, if you search after him with all your heart and with all your soul."
- ♥ Proverbs 8:17 - "I love those who love me, and those who seek me diligently find me."
- ♥ Jeremiah 29:12-14 – "Then, you will call upon me and come and pray to me, and I will hear you. You will seek me and find me, when you seek me with all your heart. I will be found by you, declares the Lord, and I will restore your fortunes and gather you from all the nations and all the places where I have driven you, declares the Lord, and I will bring you back to the place from which I sent you into exile."
- ♥ Matthew 7:7-8 - "Ask, and it will be given to you; seek, and you will find; knock, and it will be opened to you. For everyone who asks receives, and the one who seeks finds, and to the one who knocks it will be opened."

- ♥ 1 Chronicles 16:11 – "Seek the Lord and his strength; seek His presence continually!
- ♥ Lamentations 3:25 – "The Lord is good to those who wait for Him, to the soul who seeks Him."
- ♥ Isaiah 55:6-7 - "Seek the Lord while he may be found; call upon him while he is near; let the wicked forsake his way, and the unrighteous man his thoughts; let him return to the Lord, that he may have compassion on him, and to our God, for he will abundantly pardon."
- ♥ Matthew 6:33 - "But seek first the kingdom of God and His righteousness, and all these things will be added to you."
- ♥ Psalm 119:10 – "With my whole heart I seek you; let me not wander from your commandments!"
- ♥ Jeremiah 29:13 – "You will seek me and find me, when you seek me with all your heart."
- ♥ Hebrews 11:6 – "And, without faith it is impossible to please Him, for whoever would draw near to God must believe that

he exists and that He rewards those who seek Him."

Notes

_____

_____

_____

_____

_____

_____

_____

_____

_____

_____

_____

_____

_____

_____

_____

_____

_____

_____

_____

_____

_____

_____

Notes

_____

_____

_____

_____

_____

_____

_____

_____

_____

_____

_____

_____

_____

_____

_____

_____

_____

_____

_____

_____

Chapter 2
Falling in Love with Yourself

Do you love yourself? Do you *truly* love yourself? Unfortunately, most people are filled with so much insecurity and self-doubt that they can't honestly answer "yes" to that question. We, as women, are constantly comparing what we have to other women and other relationships. We're basing our happiness off what we see in their lives rather than what God hasplanned for us. If you are single, it's time to take the time to fall in love with yourself. And, I don't mean that fake, social media, I'm just faking so people won't really know the truth love... I mean real, genuine: I love myself, my big nose, my big hair, and my big thighs self!

You are so beautiful and unique. There is a reason that God created only one you. Take the time to really get to know who you are before you commit to someone else. Date yourself before you consider dating someone else. Do you know what you want in a mate? What are your likes and dislikes? Allow yourself to get to a place where you're okay with being alone. Singleness is not a curse; instead, it's a time for preparation for your husband. Live your life. Take yourself to dinner. Learn a new language. Enjoy the life that God has given you. It is indeed a blessing. Don't beat yourself up about being not being in a relationship.

Become a woman with something to offer a future mate. Simply take this time to love on yourself.

Once you begin to understand the love that God has for you, your only choice is to love yourself. "You are all together beautiful, my love;

there is no flaw in you." (Song of Solomon 4:7) Self-love creates self-worth, and knowing your worth is a beautiful thing. You begin to recognize that you don't have to settle for anything. You learn to accept the best, not just in your relationship, but in every area of your life. You are a child of God, and you only deserve the best. Understand that your father is a King. The only way you will ever truly accept His best is to honestly and truly love yourself.

One day, I was talking to a good girlfriend of mine, and she was telling me about her relationship issues. She was dating a man who was not committed to her and had no interest in being in a relationship. I had to take a moment to look her in the eyes and ask her, "Do you believe that you are truly worthy of love?" She looked at me and said, "NO!" That is when I realized that she is not the only woman that feels this way. When I hear this from a woman, it saddens me because we attract what we believe, and our thoughts become our reality. If we truly believe that we don't deserve a relationship, then the chances of it manifesting in our lives is slim to none. This is a clear indication that we must take the time to truly love ourselves.

When we don't love ourselves, we attract men who aren't good for us. These are the type of men who are drawn to and thrive off insecurity. They can smell you coming a mile away. They take advantage of your insecurities and use them to their benefit. You see, a real man isn't attracted to a woman who is insecure. He will run in the opposite direction. He's looking for a woman who is confident and has no problem letting the world know exactly who she is. Therefore, it is vital to have a relationship with God. He will allow you to discern who is worthy of your time while you are growing into the woman that you are destined to become.

There was a point in my life when I didn't truly love myself. In fact, I didn't even like myself. I put on a front for everyone because I couldn't allow the truth to be known or seen. However, once I learned about His grace and His love, I began to see myself the way God sees me. He loved me so much that He thought I was to die for. Once I understood His love for me, it changed how I loved and saw myself. In turn, I began to hold others accountable for the way they loved and treated me. I was able to unapologetically start creating boundaries for the relationship I was in, and I learned that "No." was a complete sentence. I had spent time getting to know who Shenique was, and I discovered exactly what she wanted. I didn't owe anyone an explanation. This didn't require me to be mean or rude. It was just me allowing my confidence to shine and finally knowing who and whose I was. I belong to Christ and so do you. Imagine if we all began to act as our true selves. Oh! How amazing that would be! We all are queens, and we deserve to be treated as such. I think it's time we all started acting like it.

Scriptures on Loving Yourself

- ♥ Philippians 4:13 – "I can do all things through Christ who strengthens me."
- ♥ 2 Timothy 1:7 – "For God gave us a spirit not of fear but of power and love and self-control."
- ♥ Hebrews 10:35-36 – "Therefore, do not throw away your confidence, which has a great reward. For you have need of endurance, so that when you have done the will of God you may receive what is promised."
- ♥ Hebrews 13:6 – "So we can confidently say, 'The Lord is my helper; I will not fear; what can man do to me?' "
- ♥ Joshua 1:9 – "Have I not commanded you? Be strong and courageous. Do not be frightened, and do not be dismayed, for the LORD your God is with you wherever you go."
- ♥ Psalm 139:13-14 – "For you formed my inward parts; you knitted me together in my mother's womb. I praise you, for I am fearfully and wonderfully made.

Wonderful are your works; my soul knows it very well."

- ♥ Psalm 27:3 – "Though an army encamp against me, my heart shall not fear; though war arise against me, yet I will be confident."
- ♥ Ephesians 4:29 – "Let no corrupting talk come out of your mouths, but only such as is good for building up, as fits the occasion, that it may give grace to those who hear."
- ♥ Proverbs 3:6 – "In all your ways acknowledge Him, and He will make straight your paths.
- ♥ 1 John 4:18 – "There is no fear in love, but perfect love casts out fear. For fear has to do with punishment, and whoever fears has not been perfected in love."
- ♥ Psalm 138:8 – "The LORD will fulfill his purpose for me; your steadfast love, O LORD, endures forever. Do not forsake the work of your hands."
- ♥ Philippians 4:4-7 – "Rejoice in the Lord always; again, I will say, Rejoice. Let your reasonableness be known to everyone. The Lord is at hand; do not be anxious

about anything, but in everything by prayer and supplication with thanksgiving let your requests be made known to God. And the peace of God, which surpasses all understanding, will guard your hearts and your minds in Christ Jesus."

♥ Galatians 2:20 – "I have been crucified with Christ. It is no longer I who live, but Christ who lives in me. And the life I now live in the flesh I live by faith in the Son of God, who loved me and gave himself for me."

♥ Matthew 6:34 - "Therefore do not be anxious about tomorrow, for tomorrow will be anxious for itself. Sufficient for the day is its own trouble."

Notes

_____

_____

_____

_____

_____

_____

_____

_____

_____

_____

_____

_____

_____

_____

_____

_____

_____

_____

_____

_____

_____

_____

Notes

_____

_____

_____

_____

_____

_____

_____

_____

_____

_____

_____

_____

_____

_____

_____

_____

_____

_____

_____

_____

_____

Chapter 3
Pray for Your Mate

Have you been talking to God about your mate? Have you truly taken the time to get down on your knees and pray about this man? When was the last time you strategically prayed to God about your life and the people that should be in it? We must learn to spend time with God and allow Him to direct us. We pray about our health, career, and finances, but for some reason, we exclude God when it comes to our relationships. Proverbs 3:5 says, "Trust in the LORD with all your heart and lean not to your own understanding; in all your ways acknowledge Him, and He will direct your paths." Allow Him to speak to your heart and mind about choosing the right mate. Pray for discernment, so that you will know who is worthy of having a personal relationship with you. This position is not for just anyone. God knows you because He created you. Therefore, He knows who is perfect for you. It's time to talk to Him. He will give you all the desires of your heart if you allow Him to be first in your life.

It's okay to want love, but don't focus on having a boyfriend or getting married. Take the time to focus on God and the advancement of His kingdom, and let Him take care of the rest. I have learned that if you continue to leave God out of your life and decisions, things will only get worst. In the beginning of my current relationship, I tried to do everything. I was playing God in my life. I wasn't being obedient to what He was telling me. The good news is that my relationship with God wasn't nonexistent. However, it wasn't as strong as it should have been. So, when I initially sought His guidance, He told me exactly what the deal was. The bad news is that I didn't listen. I did what Shenique wanted to do, and I had to deal with the consequences of not listening.

Now, that didn't change God's plans for me, but it did delay it. You see, our disobedience doesn't ruin His plans for us, but it does complicate them. There are consequences for all our actions. God wants you to experience heaven on earth in every area of your life. But, if you decide to go against the plans that He has for you, then you will have to deal with situations that were never intended for you.

God spoke to me and specifically told me, "Be his friend." But, you know what I did? I tried to be his girlfriend, his lover, and his wife. I was cooking, cleaning, having sex, and doing whatever I thought would make him change his mind about being with me. And, guess what? None of those things helped to change his mind. Honestly, it may sound bad, but I wasn't doing anything different from what most women do in relationships. However, I wasn't being obedient to what God was telling me to do. I was attempting to be everything but what God told me to be. I ignored what He said, and I paid for it.

I was constantly frustrated and angry with myself because no matter what I did, the relationship never worked. At that point, there was no relationship, and I had no peace whatsoever. I was insecure, and I questioned everything about myself when it came to the "relationship." There was no joy, and there was NO LOVE. This was not God's plan or intention for me, but I wasn't allowing Him to work in my life; therefore, He wasn't. I was too busy doing His job, and He was just waiting for me to move out of the way. You see, God has planned each of your seasons, and you will cause problems for yourself if you attempt to work out of season.

Furthermore, you cannot expect a harvest, if you have not planted a seed.

Looking back, I have realized that I was working out of season. Is there a chance that you may be doing the same thing? God gave me specific instructions, but I was so focused on what I wanted that I just completely ignored what He was telling me to do. He wanted us to establish a lasting relationship through friendship. However, I was focused on my own desires. I can't tell you how many times I begged and pleaded with Him to help me, but He had already answered my prayer.

Has God already answered your prayer? Are you being obedient to what He is telling you? I would go to my friends and family asking for advice and applying that to our relationship just to create more havoc and drama for myself. I was listening to everyone, focusing on my past, listening to the devils' suggestions, and ignoring what God was telling me. I remember when I would get emotional and want to do crazy things like question him or stalk his social media accounts. Then, I could hear His still voice telling me to stop. Still, I did what I wanted to do. And, it caused so much heartache in the long run. If I had been obedient to God's specific instructions, then we would have been able to enjoy the beginning stages of our relationship a lot more.

I know now that God wanted me to develop a friendship with this man before the relationship, but I was putting the carriage before the horse. I was more concerned with being in a relationship instead of trying to build one. We tend to look at romance and love as the long-term goal, but the reality is that friendship is the basis of a successful relationship. We hop in and out of bed with men having sex, and we never build the foundation of a relationship. Then, we wonder why it never works. Friendship allows clarity and authenticity to show up. Once you develop a friendship, it allows you to see who this man really is without the distraction of sex.

Praying for your mate allows God to have His hand in your relationship. He will guide you and speak to your heart on the things that you should do. He will tell you when it's time to move on from someone you're dating. He wants you to have the man of your dreams, but He must come first. I can guarantee that you will never find that man unless you can recognize that you need God more. Take a lesson from my life. I was putting the man first, and the moment I began to seek God first, everything changed. As women, we just want to be loved so badly that we risk everything to find that "love." Have you ever thought that things might not be going right because you haven't allowed God to be involved in your relationships? It's time for Him to be included.

Scriptures on Praying for a Mate

- ♥ Mark 11:24 – "Therefore I tell you, whatever you ask in prayer, believe that you have received it, and it will be yours."
- ♥ Matthew 7:7 - "Ask, and it will be given to you; seek, and you will find; knock, and it will be opened to you."
- ♥ Isaiah 34:16 – "Seek and read from the book of the LORD: Not one of these shall be missing; none shall be without her mate. For the mouth of the LORD has commanded, and his Spirit has gathered them."
- ♥ Psalm 37:4-5 – "Delight yourself in the LORD, and he will give you the desires of your heart. Commit your way to the LORD; trust in Him, and He will act."
- ♥ Genesis 2:18 – "Then the LORD God said, 'It is not good that the man should be alone; I will make him a helper fit for him.'"
- ♥ Jeremiah 29:11 – "For I know the plans I have for you, declares the LORD, plans for welfare and not for evil, to give you a future and a hope."

- Matthew 6:33 – "But seek first the kingdom of God and his righteousness, and all these things will be added to you."
- Proverbs 18:22 – "He who finds a wife finds a good thing and obtains favor from the LORD."
- Ruth 1:9 – "The LORD grant that you may find rest, each of you in the house of her husband!" Then she kissed them, and they lifted up their voices and wept."
- Romans 15:13 – "May the God of hope fill you with all joy and peace in believing, so that by the power of the Holy Spirit you may abound in hope."
- Genesis 2:24 – "Therefore, a man shall leave his father and his mother and hold fast to his wife, and they shall become one flesh."
- Matthew 21:22 – "And whatever you ask in prayer, you will receive, if you have faith."

Notes

_____

_____

_____

_____

_____

_____

_____

_____

_____

_____

_____

_____

_____

_____

_____

_____

_____

_____

_____

_____

_____

_____

Notes

_____

_____

_____

_____

_____

_____

_____

_____

_____

_____

_____

_____

_____

_____

_____

_____

_____

_____

_____

_____

_____

_____

_____

Chapter 4
Identity... Do you know who you are?

Have you ever looked at yourself in the mirror and realized who you are? Have you really taken the time to recognize that you are the daughter of a King? He knew you before you were born. He watched you in your mother's womb. God thinks you are so beautiful and amazing that you were to die for! You are a princess, but for some odd reason, you have been acting as a peasant. You have allowed men to come into your life to do whatever they want, and you have accepted it just so you won't be alone. The truth is, you've done a lot more than just entertain them. Instead, you have created the opportunity for havoc to come into your life.

When you allow drama to come into your life, you begin to take ownership of other things such as hurt, pain, and disappointment. These are all from the enemy. God never intended for you to take possession of these because He knows exactly who you are. When you begin to accept Satan's suggestions, you begin to delay God's plan for you. However, Satan has no authority over you because you are NOT his. When you were a child, did you listen to what strangers told you to do? Uh no... And, you know why you didn't? It's because you didn't belong to them. Just the same, why do you continuously allow Satan to get in your head? Newsflash! You DO NOT belong to him!

Did you know that you have more power than Satan has? He hates you because of that. Did you know that? When I found out that he hates me and wants me to fail, that changed everything for me. Did you know he wants to be us? We as children of God have more authority than Satan, and he doesn't want us to know that. When he was cast out of heaven, he lost his standing with God. So, to ensure that you don't get all those blessings he missed out on, he stays in your ear to make sure that you don't get them either. He tells you things like: "You're not good enough." "God doesn't love you." "Do you really think God is going to bless you after what you did last night?" "No one is ever going to marry you." "You're not attractive."

Do you realized that the only way he has power is if YOU give it to him? If you accept his suggestions, then you give him control over your life. Sis, I'm here to tell you that he is a LIAR! Please do not give life to his suggestions, because that's all they are. They have no truth or validity to them. You are beautiful and intelligent, and you have purpose. If you allow the devil to have power over your mind and thoughts, he wins.

Therefore, is so important to know who you are in Christ.

The Bible says in Jeremiah 1:5, "Before I formed you in the womb I knew you, before you were born I set you apart; I appointed you as a prophet of nations." The amplified version states, "Before I formed you in the womb I knew you [and approved of you as My chosen instrument], And before you were born I consecrated you [to Myself as My own]; I have appointed you as prophet to the nations." There's your proof. You were destined to be great. You were chosen by Him. It's time for us to truly know and understand who we are in Him. If we know who we are, then we can set boundaries in our relationships, whether they are romantic or platonic.

Take a moment to think of the last time you dealt with getting your heartbroken or being disappointed. Did you build an emotional wall?

Was it harder to trust others afterwards? Disappointments in relationships cause us to build walls and prevent us from being open to having a relationship with anyone. While that wall will protect you from hurt and pain, it will also keep you from the love you long for. You have got to get to a place where you allow yourself to trust God, trust yourself, and trust the process. There is a closeness that you must have with God to recognize who is worthy of your time and love. We don't have to accept the beliefs of society and apply them to our lives. We are the exception. We belong to Christ.

Why is it that we don't believe we can have the relationships of our dreams? Stop and think about this for a moment. Do you really believe that you are worthy of a healthy, loving relationship? My theory is that most women don't believe that it's possible. That's because you believe what you speak and all I hear is:

"Men are dogs." "There are no good men left." "He doesn't want *me*." "Men always do me wrong." "I will never find anyone." "I will never find love." Well guess what, sis? You are right. Whatever you think will come to pass. How do you expect to experience a successful relationship if all you are ever speaking is the exact opposite of what you really want?

Remember that death and life are in the power of the tongue. You are speaking your life into existence. Consequently, your life will go in the direction of what you think. You have begun to believe what society tells you, yet they aren't the author of your life. God is the author of your life, and you only need to apply to your life what He says. The devil wants you believe that you aren't what God says you are. So, he uses statistics, what people say, and your insecurities against you. Society (also know as the devil) often says things like: "Why aren't you married? What's wrong with you?" "You are 30 and single. What's wrong with you?" "I have been single for two years. What's wrong with me?" Well it's time to tell the devil to take his suggestions and leave you alone!

My issue was that I listened to all those things. I was thirty years old, coming out of a five-year relationship with a man who didn't want to get married, and I was walking into one with a man who didn't want a relationship. Oh Lord! Help me! But remember, He told me to be his friend, but I let my past and what everyone else was saying affect me. I did not recognize my identity. I took every suggestion that the devil handed me. "No one will ever marry you." "Your father isn't around; no man will ever respect a woman whose father isn't around." "You're not good enough to be someone's wife." How many of you have or are experiencing this? Rebuke the devil and get on with your life! His ole whack butt will try to attack our weak spots. But, he has no authority over us whatsoever. We need to start putting him in his place and out of our life!

Scriptures on Identity

- ♥ Genesis 1:27 – "So God created man in His own image, in the image of God he created him; male and female he created them."

- ♥ Jeremiah 1:5 - "Before I formed you in the womb I knew you, and before you were born I consecrated you; I appointed you a prophet to the nations."

- ♥ 2 Corinthians 5:17 – "Therefore, if anyone is in Christ, he is a new creation. The old has passed away; behold, the new has come."

- ♥ 1 Peter 2:9 – "But you are a chosen race, a royal priesthood, a holy nation, a people for his own possession, that you may proclaim the excellencies of him who called you out of darkness into his marvelous light."

- ♥ Galatians 2:20 – "I have been crucified with Christ. It is no longer I who live, but Christ who lives in me. And the life I now live in the flesh I live by faith in the Son of God, who loved me and gave himself for me."

- ♥ 1 John 3:1-3 – "See what kind of love the Father has given to us, that we should be called children of God; and so, we are. The reason why the world does not know us is that it did not know Him. Beloved, we are God's children now, and what we will be has not yet appeared; but we know that when He appears we shall be like Him, because we shall see Him as He is. And everyone who thus hopes in Him purifies Himself as He is pure."

- ♥ 1 Corinthians 6:19-20 – "Or do you not know that your body is a temple of the Holy Spirit within you, whom you have from God? You are not your own, for you were bought with a price. So, glorify God in your body."

- ♥ Colossians 3:1-4 – "If then you have been raised with Christ, seek the things that are above, where Christ is, seated at the right hand of God. Set your minds on things that are above, not on things that are on earth. For you have died, and your life is hidden with Christ in God. When Christ who is your life appears, then you also will appear with Him in glory."

- ♥ Ephesians 2:10 ESV – "For we are his workmanship, created in Christ Jesus for good works, which God prepared beforehand, that we should walk in them."
- ♥ John 15:15 – "No longer do I call you servants, for the servant does not know what his master is doing; but I have called you friends, for all that I have heard from my Father I have made known to you."
- ♥ Ephesians 4:22-24 – "To put off your old self, which belongs to your former manner of life and is corrupt through deceitful desires, and to be renewed in the spirit of your minds, and to put on the new self, created after the likeness of God in true righteousness and holiness."
- ♥ John 15:5 – "I am the vine; you are the branches. Whoever abides in me and I in Him, He it is that bears much fruit, for apart from me you can do nothing."

Notes

_____

_____

_____

_____

_____

_____

_____

_____

_____

_____

_____

_____

_____

_____

_____

_____

_____

_____

_____

_____

_____

Notes

_____

_____

_____

_____

_____

_____

_____

_____

_____

_____

_____

_____

_____

_____

_____

_____

_____

_____

_____

_____

_____

Chapter 5
Understand God's Love for You

Now that you've taken the time to talk to God and learn more about your identity, the next step is to understand God's love for you. Do you know how special you are to Him? Do you know that He chose you? Psalm 139:13 says, "For you did form my inward parts. You did knit me together in my mother's womb." WOW! How amazing is that? He made you, and He considers you His masterpiece. What artist doesn't love their masterpiece?   He spent time on you, and He perfected every single part of your body. He put the features of your face and the hairs on your head together. Every small detail about you was created personally by Him. He did this all because He loves you. YOU! He sent His son to die for your sins. (Past, present and future). He gave you the gift of grace so that no matter what mistakes you made, you would be forgiven. There is nothing that you can do to stop Him from loving you. Understand that He loves you enough to provide you with a mate that will love, respect and cherish you.

Have there been times when you felt like God was punishing you for something you did before and that's why you haven't found someone? I believe that sometimes we mentally punish ourselves because we think that God has taken something away from us in the present to punish us for something we did in our past. I mean, let's be honest. Do you believe that God hasn't sent your mate because of something trifling you did when you were twenty-two or twenty-three? Well, I'm here to tell you that you're wrong.

God is a loving God, and He wants the best for you. However, we must understand that there are always consequences for our actions. That's why God created a certain way to live, based on what He teaches us in the bible. That is how He illustrates His love for us through His word. You see, God never intended for us to deal with hurt, pain, or disappointment. He loves us way too much for that. God wants us to continuously set our eyes on Him. He wants to order our steps and direct our paths. These are all the ways that He expresses His love for us.

Sis, I want to stress to you how important this is to your process in finding love and experiencing a life full of prosperity. God loves you so much that He allowed His son to be crucified just to save you. As a parent, could you imagine allowing your innocent child to be sacrificed for the sins of someone else? That's just what God did for us. Let's stop and think about that for a moment… Isn't that an amazing feeling? It takes my breath away just thinking it and writing this to you. Knowing who you are in Christ is fully accepting His love for you. That also means that you have to be willing to accept His plans for you.

As women, when we accept Christ's' love, we must deny the thoughts of the enemy (Satan). The enemy will try to convince you that you are not worthy of love and commitment, and he will even try to rob you of your self-esteem with his propositions. Satan's whole goal is to make you believe that God and his word are not true. If I can stress anything more to you, DO NOT BELIEVE him. He IS A LIAR. God loves you so much. Can I say that one more time? GOD LOVES YOU SO MUCH!

When I began to seek God, I had to learn about His love and grace first. You see, that determines what I accept from myself and others. In the past, I would allow the devil to have his way with my thoughts and my actions. I had no self-esteem. Moreover, I didn't believe that God loved me because I only saw Him as a punishing God. That's what religion had taught me my whole life. When my pastor began to teach on grace, it gave me a totally different view on who God was and what our relationship should look like. I began to see Him as a more loving and nurturing God. After that, I began to spend time with Him. I began to worship Him. I began to understand His word when I would read it. (Remember, if you have a hard time reading the bible and understanding it, I suggest purchasing a study bible. The NIV version is easier to read than the King James version).

As I got closer to Him, I began to view myself differently. I started to fully accept who I was, mistakes and imperfections included. I had lied to myself for so long that it was time for me to start being honest. That is when the hard part started. Not only did God expose His love for me, but He also exposed the things that I needed to correct within myself. I had dealt with so many dysfunctional relationships in the past that I still carried a lot of old habits, and it was time for me to get rid of them. Have you heard that it's hard to teach an old dog new tricks? Well, it's true because this "old dog" struggled to get rid of her old ways.

God revealed to me that it was time for me to stop shooting myself in the foot due to negative thoughts and wrong believing. Are you still so caught up in your past that you don't allow anyone in? You're so busy stalking a female's or an ex-boyfriend's social media that you can't even fully enjoy who is standing in front of you? Maybe you're that girl that a man has to be so "perfect" for you that the moment you see a flaw, you drop him. These are all examples of how Satan tries to trick you into living a lie. Your past is behind you and cannot affect your future. Let it go. Watching your ex's or someone else's life only hinders you from reaching your full potential. God loves you so much that even if you are dealing with any of these circumstances, He will help you overcome them. Satan will allow these situations to overtake you and your circumstance is NOT who you are. God wants you to enjoy life. He wants to shower you with his love but the only way he can do that is if you allow him to. Take the time to get to know him and his plans for you.

Scriptures on God's Love for You

- ♥ John 3:16 - "For God so loved the world, that He gave his only Son, that whoever believes in Him should not perish but have eternal life."
- ♥ 1 John 3:1 – "See what kind of love the Father has given to us, that we should be called children of God; and so, we are. The reason why the world does not know us is that it did not know Him."
- ♥ Hebrews 13:8 – "Jesus Christ is the same yesterday and today and forever."
- ♥ John 17:26 – "I made known to them your name, and I will continue to make it known, that the love with which you have loved me may be in them, and I in them."
- ♥ Titus 3:5 – "He saved us, not because of works done by us in righteousness, but according to His own mercy, by the washing of regeneration and renewal of the Holy Spirit."
- ♥ Romans 10:9 – "Because, if you confess with your mouth that Jesus is Lord and believe in your heart that God raised Him from the dead, you will be saved."

- ♥ Romans 5:8 – "But God shows his love for us in that while we were still sinners, Christ died for us."
- ♥ John 10:10 – "The thief comes only to steal and kill and destroy. I came that they may have life and have it abundantly."
- ♥ 1 John 4:8 – "Anyone who does not love does not know God, because God is love."
- ♥ 1 Peter 2:24 – "He himself bore our sins in his body on the tree, that we might die to sin and live to righteousness. By his wounds, you have been healed."
- ♥ Ephesians 3:14-19 – "For this reason I bow my knees before the Father, from whom every family in heaven and on earth is named, that according to the riches of his glory He may grant you to be strengthened with power through his Spirit in your inner being, so that Christ may dwell in your hearts through faith— that you, being rooted and grounded in love, may have strength to comprehend with all the saints what is the breadth and length and height and depth."
- ♥ John 17:23 – "I in them and you in me, that they may become perfectly one, so

that the world may know that you sent me and loved them even as you loved me."

- ♥ John 13:1 – "Now before the Feast of the Passover, when Jesus knew that His hour had come to depart out of this world to the Father, having loved His own who were in the world, He loved them to the end."
- ♥ Psalm 46:10 - "Be still, and know that I am God. I will be exalted among the nations, I will be exalted in the earth!"
- ♥ 1 John 2:5 – "But whoever keeps His word, in Him truly the love of God is perfected. By this we may know that we are in Him."
- ♥ John 16:27 – "For the Father himself loves you, because you have loved me and have believed that I came from God."
- ♥ John 15:13 – "Greater love has no one than this, that someone lay down His life for His friends."

Notes

Notes

Chapter 6
Letting Go of Your Past

Remember when I mentioned that Satan loves to make suggestions to get into your head? Well, here we have exhibit A... *Your past.* Oh, he loves to use your past to convince you that you aren't worthy of whatever it is you are asking God for. Let's think about it for a second. What's keeping you from fulfilling your dreams right now? It's probably fear. But, where does that fear derive from? Was it that time you got your heart broken? *Your past.* Maybe it was that time you tried to start a business and it failed. *Your past.* Did it come from the fact that your father wasn't in your life as a child? *Your past.* How about that time you got cheated on? Y*our past.*

I get it. You don't want to be hurt. You don't want to be disappointed. You definitely don't want your heart broken again. No one wants to be vulnerable and jeopardize their personal or professional life. However, I would bet my salary that you are more willing to take risks in your career a lot faster than you would take with your heart. Nevertheless, the reality is that you will never get to where you want to be without taking a risk. The bigger the risk, the greater the reward. BUT, I have good news. God took care of that as well. He has given you your personal GPS... the Holy Spirit. The Holy Spirit is there to give you direction. It is our responsibility to develop a relationship with God so that when the Holy Spirit speaks, we can hear Him clearly and obey Him.

When it comes to relationships we never want to be hurt or disappointed by the ones we love. It just doesn't feel good to have your heart broken, but see that's why we have God. He gives us peace in the middle of a storm. Keep in mind that once that storm is over, you shouldn't continue to dwell in it. Use that time to learn from your situation and move on. Our past should not hinder us from our present or our future. We allow just the thought of the past to get us worked up, and the next thing we know, we're going the opposite direction of where we should be headed. The Bible says, "Do not be anxious about anything, but in every situation, by prayer and petition, with thanksgiving, present your requests to God. And the peace of God, which transcends all understanding, will guard your hearts and your minds in Christ Jesus." (Philippians 4:6-7)

Sis! Do you know the power you have at your fingertips? We have the authority to make our requests known to God. Pray about the situation, pray for your ex - or whoever hurt you- and let it go. Don't be so focused on the pain that the last person caused, that you delay having the relationship that God himself has prepared for you. Don't torture yourself. It is time to forgive your ex and forgive yourself. That person wasn't for you. So, don't let bitterness and resentment deter you from being the person God has created you to be. He has someone so special for you, and He knows exactly what you want and exactly what you need. Their rejection is His protection. He is setting you up something great. Trust Him.

When I was growing up, my mother and father were not together. I never really knew what a healthy relationship looked like. I just had my friends and other family members' relationships to view as examples. I always had dreams of being swept off my feet by the man who I loved, but I didn't know what love should look like. I didn't know how a man should pursue a woman or what he was supposed to do when he really cared for a woman. Consequently, if a man gave me the amount of attention that I thought was sufficient, I would entertain him. Now, I wasn't "fast" as the old folks would say. However, I will say that I dealt with a lot of other issues within my relationships because of low self-esteem and because I did not know my worth.

My father wasn't there to tell me what I deserved or that I was beautiful. Therefore, for a long time, I was angry at him and my mother. I was angry because he wasn't there for me, and I felt like it was his fault that I had so many relationships issues. I was angry at my mother because I felt like she could have chosen a better father for me. I had to come to a point where I realized that my parents were only human. As young immigrants, they did the best they could do. I had to take responsibility of my life and stop blaming them for my issues.

When I began to get into long term relationships as an adult, there were many things that I accepted from the men that I would date. I wanted to be loved and thought that I could, in so many ways, convince them to love me. I accepted cheating, verbal abuse, and stagnancy within my relationships. I was so afraid to lose them. However, the truth is they were never intended for me in the first place. So, do you see what happens? We deal with relationships that were never for us, and it hurts us in the long run.

I have only been in three long-term relationships as an adult, and I knew all along throughout the first two that I had no business hanging on as long I did. Does that sound familiar? I was so afraid of being alone that I made excuses for why things were not going as I imagined. I truly believe that, as women, we know when it's time to let go. Still, there's a big difference in knowing and doing. We can make or break who we are based on the amount of dysfunction we accept from our mate. God may allow us to experience things to make us strong. Yet, when we stay in it past our expiration date, that's when things can become dangerous.

Now, you've been in a relationship multiple years. You've been abused and taken advantage of, and you no longer have any self-esteem because you can't figure out why he treats you the way he does. You often ask yourself: Why won't he commit to me? Why won't he just love me? Why does he cheat on me? Why won't he marry me? God has put all the signs in front of you. He has told you to leave time after time, but you won't listen. So, guess what, sis? You are going to have to deal with the consequences of being disobedient. You are so afraid of starting all over, right? You believe that no one else will make you "feel" the way he does.

You won't love another person the way you love him, right? WRONG.

God is just waiting for you to let go so that He can work for you. But, you're so busy playing God that He moves out of the way. I heard someone say once, "God is a gentleman. He will move out the way for you." God's not going to compete with you when you won't allow Him to work on your behalf. You must trust Him enough to either correct your situation or create a new one for you. When you don't allow God to work for you, and you become disobedient, it puts you in a place where your heart becomes hardened. I think we all have experienced heartbreak, so let's stop and think for a minute about what that does to us... So, what did you come up with? You put your guards up. You might not be as nice of a person as you were before your heartbreak occurred. What else? You have become more reserved and closed off, right? Exactly!

Well, God is sending your husband your way. Meanwhile, you are emotionally scarred because you allowed someone who was never meant for you to come in and literally shake things up. Therefore, it is so important to let go of your past. Don't get me wrong, it won't be easy. You'll have to break those old habits and change the way you think. All those things that you learned in your dysfunctional relationship, should cease. There will be no more checking phones and social media, because with the right one, you won't have to do those things. There will be no more creating drama, because the right one won't come with any. There will be no more need to see if he's lying, because with the right one, you will have trust.

I'm not saying he'll be perfect (we'll talk about that a little later), but I am saying you will have peace with the man you are supposed to be with. You'll be able to trust him, and you will know where you stand in his life. He'll be clear and direct about what he wants from you. Just understand that our past does not determine who we are, or who we will become, in our personal life or in our professional life. Our parents, exes, and society no longer have control of whether we get married or not. You make the decision. Simply, give God permission to act on your behalf within your relationships, and let the past go. We all can learn from it, but don't allow it to change the person that He intended you to be. Don't give consent to having anger and bitterness control you because of what happened with the last guy. Leave your past exactly where it is, in the past.

Scriptures on Letting Go of your Past

- ♥ Philippians 4:6-7 – "Do not be anxious about anything, but in everything by prayer and supplication with thanksgiving let your requests be made known to God. And the peace of God, which surpasses all understanding, will guard your hearts and your minds in Christ Jesus."
- ♥ Ephesians 4:31 – "Let all bitterness and wrath and anger and clamor and slander be put away from you, along with all malice."
- ♥ Proverbs 3:5 – "Trust in the Lord with all your heart, and do not lean on your own understanding."
- ♥ Matthew 6:14 – "For if you forgive others their trespasses, your heavenly Father will also forgive you."
- ♥ Romans 12:19 – "Beloved, never avenge yourselves, but leave it to the wrath of God, for it is written, 'Vengeance is mine, I will repay, says the Lord.'"
- ♥ Matthew 5:44 – "But I say to you, 'Love your enemies and pray for those who persecute you.'"

- ♥ 1 Peter 5:6-7 – "Humble yourselves, therefore, under the mighty hand of God so that at the proper time He may exalt you, casting all your anxieties on Him, because He cares for you."
- ♥ Ephesians 4:26-27 – "Be angry and do not sin; do not let the sun go down on your anger, and give no opportunity to the devil."
- ♥ Proverbs 15:1 – "A soft answer turns away wrath, but a harsh word stirs up anger."
- ♥ Philippians 4:7 – "And the peace of God, which surpasses all understanding, will guard your hearts and your minds in Christ Jesus."
- ♥ 2 Timothy 2:23-26 – "Have nothing to do with foolish, ignorant controversies; you know that they breed quarrels. And the Lord's servant must not be quarrelsome but kind to everyone, able to teach, patiently enduring evil, correcting his opponents with gentleness. God may perhaps grant them repentance leading to a knowledge of the truth, and they may come to their senses and escape from the

snare of the devil, after being captured by Him to do His will."

♥ Philippians 4:6 – "Do not be anxious about anything, but in everything by prayer and supplication with thanksgiving let your requests be made known to God."

Notes

Notes

_____

_____

_____

_____

_____

_____

_____

_____

_____

_____

_____

_____

_____

_____

_____

_____

_____

_____

_____

_____

_____

_____

Chapter 7
God Created a Specific Lane Just for You

As I've grown, I have learned that our society is too focused on competition. We sometimes lose sight of our blessings because we are too fixated on what someone else has. We see another woman, and we like her hair or like what she's wearing. However, we are so used to competing that we immediately become jealous of her instead of simply complimenting her. What's up with that? I don't know if it hasn't been said or maybe we're accustomed to old habits, but NEWS FLASH... You both can be cute. Just because she has on a nice dress and her hair looks nice doesn't take anything away from you. There's enough opportunity and supplies in the world for you both to win!

Y'all might get mad at me on this one, but this is a subject that I must address. Ladies, WE MUST STOP COMPETING WITH EACH OTHER. Whew! I had to get that off my chest. No, seriously... Why are we so mad at one another? Why do we compete for men? I asked myself this question when I pondered over the fact that there are so many women who accept the role of being the "other woman." I can honestly say that I've been told by multiple women to "go get your man" or "if you don't do it someone else will." What about you? The closer I get to God, I realize that He has created a specific path for each of us. We don't have to share anything, if we don't want to do so.

I'll be honest, as a young girl, I played the role of the other woman with an ex-boyfriend. I truly believed that his new girlfriend was intruding on my territory. He was mine, and I was going to do any and everything to make sure that she didn't take what was mine. You see, I didn't love myself at all, and I wasn't at a place in life where I could be honest. Instead of leaving him alone, I decided to play a position that was an insult to who God intended for me to just so I wouldn't "lose" him. The truth is that the moment I stepped into those shoes, I had already lost. I was so full of pride that I wasn't even willing to admit I was wrong at the time. Ha! How silly of me! I had to eventually swallow my pride and apologize to that woman because I was wrong on so many levels.

How many of us are willing to admit when we are wrong in those types of situations? Once again, I allowed the devil to suggest God's promises weren't going to come to pass, and I acted out of character because of fear. I believed the enemy when he told me, "If you're not with him, you'll never find someone." Don't allow fear to come in and change who you are. That goes for any area of your life. God has created a specific lane just for you. There is no one who can take anything away from you. No one can take YOUR man, and no one can take love away from you. If they do, then it was not for you. Do you understand that? What God has for YOU is for YOU.

How many times have you been in a relationship and it ended abruptly? He started dating someone else and now you're angry and hurt. Yet, instead of blaming him, you blame her. "She stole my man! That was supposed to be my life!" You begin to focus so much on her that you forget what he did to you. Does that sound familiar? How many of us have done this? You begin to hold on to that pain and resentment forever. On the other hand, the moment you realize that he was never intended for you, you open the door for your happily ever after. We must understand that even when a relationship doesn't work, God is going to provide the right man. That doesn't mean that your ex is a bad person. Furthermore, that doesn't mean that the woman he ends up with is a horrible woman. He may be a great man, but he just may not be a great man for you - and that is okay!

Look at it like a job. Some jobs require you to be detail oriented and a team player, and others require you to be sales-driven with the ability to work alone. The person who is a team player won't qualify for the job that requires you to work alone, but does that mean you're not a good worker? Not at all! Does that mean that you're not valuable? Absolutely not! It just means that you don't qualify for that specific job. We sometimes get so caught up in "losing" that we don't see that their rejection is God's protection, and that His intentions are to bless us with our own.

Depending on how many people you date throughout life, you will "lose" someone at some point. However, that loss is only preparation for you to win the one that God created specifically for you. How amazing is that? He has created a man that brings out the best in you -one who pushes you closer God. He will love you and all your ways. If you allow God to have His way, He will provide a man that is everything you need. I think we all would prefer a man that God created specifically for each of us, rather than someone who's just filling in for the time being.

I once read an article that talked about how women are more productive when we work together. I truly believe that. Sadly, though, we let our insecurities take over, and we become enemies instead of teammates. In addition to working with other women, we must also respect one another's relationships. We can no longer knowingly date and associate with men who are dealing with, in a relationship with, or are married to another woman. It's a disservice to both you and the woman he's married to or dating. We all deserve to be in a monogamous relationship. It's time for us to stop allowing men to get away with having their cake and eating it, too. If there is a relationship, respect it (regardless of what he tells you). Just hold him accountable and walk away. That will save you from so much heartache and drama in the long run. Just remember, one day you will have a boyfriend that will eventually become your husband. You will want someone to respect your relationship as well. We must begin to be more selfless to improve self.

Scriptures on The Plans that God Has for Our Life

- ♥ Jeremiah 29:11 – "For I know the plans I have for you, declares the LORD, plans for welfare and not for evil, to give you a future and a hope."
- ♥ Proverbs 3:5-6 – "Trust in the LORD with all your heart, and do not lean on your own understanding. In all your ways acknowledge him, and He will make straight your paths."
- ♥ Romans 8:28 – "And we know that for those who love God all things work together for good, for those who are called according to His purpose."
- ♥ Ecclesiastes 3:1-22 – "For everything there is a season, and a time for every matter under heaven: a time to be born, and a time to die; a time to plant, and a time to pluck up what is planted; a time to kill, and a time to heal; a time to break down, and a time to build up; a time to weep, and a time to laugh; a time to mourn, and a time to dance; a time to cast away stones, and a time to gather

stones together; a time to embrace, and a time to refrain from embracing;"

- ♥ Proverbs 16:9 – "The heart of man plans his way, but the LORD establishes His steps."
- ♥ Isaiah 58:11 – "And the LORD will guide you continually and satisfy your desire in scorched places and make your bones strong; and you shall be like a watered garden, like a spring of water, whose waters do not fail."
- ♥ Jeremiah 1:5 - "Before I formed you in the womb I knew you, and before you were born I consecrated you; I appointed you a prophet to the nations."
- ♥ Romans 12:2 – "Do not be conformed to this world, but be transformed by the renewal of your mind, that by testing you may discern what is the will of God, what is good and acceptable and perfect."
- ♥ Psalm 27:14 – "Wait for the LORD; be strong, and let your heart take courage; wait for the LORD!"
- ♥ Psalm 32:8 – "I will instruct you and teach you in the way you should go; I will counsel you with my eye upon you."

- ♥ 1 Corinthians 2:9 – "But, as it is written, 'What no eye has seen, nor ear heard, nor the heart of man imagined, what God has prepared for those who love Him.'"
- ♥ Proverbs 19:21 – "Many are the plans in the mind of a man, but it is the purpose of the LORD that will stand."
- ♥ Psalm 37:23 – "The steps of a man are established by the LORD, when He delights in His way."
- ♥ John 15:7 – "If you abide in me, and my words abide in you, ask whatever you wish, and it will be done for you."

Notes

_____

_____

_____

_____

_____

_____

_____

_____

_____

_____

_____

_____

_____

_____

_____

_____

_____

_____

_____

_____

_____

Notes

_____

_____

_____

_____

_____

_____

_____

_____

_____

_____

_____

_____

_____

_____

_____

_____

_____

_____

_____

_____

_____

Chapter 8
Call Those Things That Be Not

I understand that sometimes it may be hard to trust the plans that God has for you. It's easy to get caught up in comparing your life to someone else's. However, you don't know what that person has dealt with to maintain their lifestyle. So, this chapter is especially for my girls. As I have stated in some of my posts and videos, I call you all my girls because we are in the same company. I understand your struggle. I have cried many nights, while begging God to fix relationship after relationship. I have watched many friends and associates live happily ever after, wondering when my day was going to come. I have had my heart broken by the man I thought I was going to spend the rest of my life with. I have sat on the phone with my friends for hours on end, hoping that one day they will give me the right advice to help make my relationship finally work. Please understand that this is coming from a place of love, and understand so I had to make sure that I included this chapter just for you.

Let's be honest here... As you begin to walk with God, you will have many obstacles. The devil comes to kill, steal, and destroy... That's his plan for you, but God has something so much better. Unfortunately, we have a bad habit of agreeing with the devil's plan before we even consider God's plan for us. You literally sign for the devil's package when you say things like: "I'm never getting married." "All men are dogs." "I'm never going to find someone who loves me." I'm here to tell you that if you truly believe these things, then that is what your reality is going to be. A good friend of mine told me a long time ago that thoughts become things. Whatever you think and believe will become physical. Yet, you have the power to control what manifests in your life based on what you think, and more so, based on what comes out of your mouth. Sis, you have the power, and it's time to use it! Life and death are in the power of the tongue. What are you speaking over your life?

I know that once you have had your heart broken so many times, it's easier to hope for the worst. You feel like this prevents you from being hurt. It's like you prepare for it so that it won't catch you off guard. Self-preservation is the worst place to be. It prevents you from being the woman that God intended for you to be. You're just not a fun person to be around, and no one wants to be in a relationship with that type of person. You have to allow yourself to trust God and let Him do the work for you. Once you begin to know your identity, let go of your past, understand His love, walk the path that He created for you, and get close to Him. Once that closeness occurs, you can discern who is worthy of your time.

Let's be clear, when you have a relationship with God you do not have to search for anything. God will put it in your face, but you must give Him permission to act on your behalf. This is where the words you speak come into play. Romans 4:17 says, "As it written, I have made you a father of many nations, in the sight of Him in whom he believed, that is, God who give life to the dead and calls into being that which does not exist." Here's your proof. You have the authority to change your life. I challenge to start using the word to your advantage. Those are His promises, so you can hold God accountable to what His word says... He's waiting for you to do so.

When you pray, thank Him before what you're praying for comes to pass in your life. Here's an example: "Lord, your word says that by His stripes I am healed. So, I thank you for healing my body." Do you see how simple that is? Of course, your senses will fight this! The things you see, hear, feel, and touch will tell you something different from what you are asking God for. Still, begin to declare now that you have a husband and that you are married, even if you don't have a prospect in sight. His word says to call those things that be not as though they were, so you have to consistently check your negative thoughts at the door. Allow God to have His way, so that you can have the desires of your heart. Renew your mind with the word. Do not allow the devil to have any leeway with your mind. Get your mind right now! Your life literally depends on it.

In June of 2013, my pastor began to preach on confirmations and how to declare the things that you were praying for over your life. During that sermon series, I wrote down everything that I was praying for, and I began to declare them every night before I said my prayers. There were nights when I would be in tears or feeling so foolish about the fact that I saw no evidence of what I was saying in my life. I was struggling financially. I was in a situation with a man who didn't want to be in a relationship with me. I hated my job. I didn't have any peace in my life. Once I began to say those confessions, my life began to shift. It was really hard at first, because I had to retrain what I had learned my whole life. I had to check the negative thoughts, and I began to watch the words that came out of my mouth like a hawk.

The more I began to trust God and get close to Him, my confidence in Him grew. By the end of 2014, I was in a committed relationship, my finances were looking up, and I had moved into a new place that I loved. In the beginning of 2015, I rewrote the confessions. This time, I added scriptures. I went through the topical bible and found a scripture on everything that I was struggling with. I even changed the way I prayed. I began to thank Him for what He had already done. I was thanking Him for a new job. In April of 2015, I got a new job - with a very nice pay increase. I was thanking Him for a new car. In May of 2015, I received a new car. This is my testimony, but I'm only writing this book because God wants you to know that whatever it is that you're are holding in your heart can also be your reality. You just have to believe.

Scriptures on the Power of the Tongue

♥ Psalm 107:2 – "Let the redeemed of the Lord say so, whom He has delivered from the hand of the adversary."

- ♥ Proverbs 18:21 – "Death and life are in the power of the tongue, and those who love it will eat its fruits."
- ♥ 1 Peter 3:10 – "For whoever desires to love life and see good days, let him keep His tongue from evil and His lips from speaking deceit."
- ♥ Ephesians 4:29 – "Let no corrupting talk come out of your mouths, but only such as is good for building up, as fits the occasion, that it may give grace to those who hear."
- ♥ Psalm 118:5 – "Out of my distress I called on the LORD; the LORD answered me and set me free."
- ♥ Psalm 141:3 – "Set a guard, O LORD, over my mouth; keep watch over the door of my lips!"
- ♥ Proverbs 15:28 – "The heart of the righteous ponders how to answer, but the mouth of the wicked pours out evil things."
- ♥ Proverbs 15:4 – "A gentle tongue is a tree of life, but perverseness in it breaks the spirit."

- ♥ Proverbs 12:18 – "There is one whose rash words are like sword thrusts, but the tongue of the wise brings healing."
- ♥ Psalm 19:14 – "Let the words of my mouth and the meditation of my heart be acceptable in your sight, O LORD, my rock and my redeemer."
- ♥ James 1:19 – "Know this, my beloved brothers: let every person be quick to hear, slow to speak, slow to anger."

Notes

_____

_____

_____

_____

_____

_____

_____

_____

_____

_____

_____

_____

_____

_____

_____

_____

_____

_____

_____

_____

_____

_____

Notes

_____

_____

_____

_____

_____

_____

_____

_____

_____

_____

_____

_____

_____

_____

_____

_____

_____

_____

_____

_____

_____

_____

Chapter 9
Trust God's Timing

As you begin to grow and develop your relationship with God, you will begin to see that the biggest part of your relationship will be trust. Unlike your mother or father, God isn't physical. Therefore, your trust in Him is developed through the faith of the unseen. That's why it's so important to work on this relationship first before ever attempting to start one with someone else. The two most vital relationships are between you and God and the one you have with yourself. It is so important to be able to love self, but you truly don't know how to do that until you know and understand God's love. His timing for what he has planned for your life is perfect.

I decided to write this book because over the past five years of my life, my relationship with God completely changed. During that change, He revealed to me some of the mistakes that women tend to make in relationships. He showed me that I had to correct some things about myself to get where I wanted to be, while still trusting His timing. We must get into a place where we are learning and progressing through each season of our lives. There are so many steps that go into preparing for a season before you ever see a harvest. The ground must be ready before you're able to plant seed in it. God is taking time to prepare your husband, but he is also preparing you.

Habakkuk 2:3 reads, "For the revelation awaits an appointed time; it speaks of the end and will not prove false. Though it lingers, wait for it; it will certainly come and will not delay." You see, there is a season for every part of your relationship. The most important is the beginning when you are establishing a friendship. You must be able to remain in that season long enough to build a solid foundation. Remember that you want a lifelong marriage, straight out the crockpot not the microwave. I'm sure you have witnessed many divorces, and that isn't what you want. Marriage is not an easy task, which is why you must be with the right person for it to last. Just let God do His work; I guarantee you won't regret it. Remember Matthew 19:6, "Since they are no longer two but one, let no one split apart what God has joined together."

Being single is also a season. You must use this time to enjoy who you are and work on just being better every day. That time can be spent working out, traveling, trying new foods or starting a business. I recommend you take this time to become the woman you want to be. If you have certain expectations of your mate while in a relationship, then it important to also have those same expectations for yourself. Take this time to become the person you want to date in a relationship. And, know that there is nothing wrong with being single. In fact, the same way that you are blessed to be married, you are blessed to be single.

Don't allow society to tell you that being single is a curse. God can use you as a single or a married woman. These are both areas of ministry that need great women to be used in them. When you are married and begin to have children, you will never be alone again. It's important to understand being single does not mean that something is wrong with you. God has already called you a wife, so you don't need a man to make you one. Use this single time to develop a better wife and mother for your family.

In my personal experience, there were times when I was frustrated because I couldn't see where my life was going or how things were going to work out. It seemed as if everyone else was getting married, having children or starting their life, except me. Once I made the decision to start learning to trust God, my first step was to consistently start tithing. If I gave the Kingdom of God the first 10% of my salary then God would provide for me and allow the 90% to take care of everything else I needed. Proverbs3:9-10 says "Honor the Lord with your wealth and with the first fruits of all your produce; then your barns will be filled with plenty, and your vats will be bursting with wine." The more that I put Him first, the more I saw my life change. It was as if God began to have a hand in everything I touched. I started to get clarity and peace within each situation I encountered. The more I sought God, the more I began to trust Him and His timing. He pressed pause on my love life and told me to redirect my focus. He was taking the time to correct everything that I had messed up. The foundation that was created was better than anything I could have done on my own, trust me I tried. If I would have rushed and forced my relationship at the wrong time (in my timing), it wouldn't have worked out and I would have been worst off. The best decision I made was to wait on God.

Only God knows exactly what we need, exactly when we need it. He knows you better than anyone else, and He knows all the intricate details of what your heart desires. Take the time to get to know Him. I promise you won't regret it.

Scriptures on God's Timing

- ♥ Habakkuk 2:3 – "For still the vision awaits its appointed time; it hastens to the end— it will not lie. If it seems slow, wait for it; it will surely come; it will not delay."
- ♥ Psalm 27:14 – "Wait for the LORD; be strong, and let your heart take courage; wait for the LORD!"
- ♥ Isaiah 40:31 – "But they who wait for the LORD shall renew their strength; they shall mount up with wings like eagles; they shall run and not be weary; they shall walk and not faint."
- ♥ Ecclesiastes 8:6 – "For there is a time and a way for everything, although man's trouble lies heavy on Him."
- ♥ Ecclesiastes 3:1 – "For everything there is a season, and a time for every matter under heaven."
- ♥ Proverbs 3:5-6 – "Trust in the LORD with all your heart, and do not lean on your own understanding. In all your ways acknowledge Him, and He will make straight your paths."

- ♥ Galatians 6:9 – "And, let us not grow weary of doing good, for in due season we will reap, if we do not give up."
- ♥ 2 Peter 3:8 – "But do not overlook this one fact, beloved, that with the Lord one day is as a thousand years, and a thousand years as one day."
- ♥ Psalm 37:3-4 – "Trust in the LORD, and do good; dwell in the land and befriend faithfulness. Delight yourself in the LORD, and he will give you the desires of your heart."
- ♥ Luke 18:27 – "But he said, 'What is impossible with men is possible with God.'"
- ♥ Lamentations 3:25-26 – "The LORD is good to those who wait for him, to the soul who seeks him. It is good that one should wait quietly for the salvation of the LORD."
- ♥ Ecclesiastes 3:11 – "He has made everything beautiful in its time. Also, he has put eternity into man's heart, yet so that he cannot find out what God has done from the beginning to the end."

♥ Genesis 18:14 – "Is anything too hard for the LORD? At the appointed time, I will return to you, about this time next year, and Sarah shall have a son."

Notes

_____

_____

_____

_____

_____

_____

_____

_____

_____

_____

_____

_____

_____

_____

_____

_____

_____

_____

_____

_____

_____

Notes

_____

_____

_____

_____

_____

_____

_____

_____

_____

_____

_____

_____

_____

_____

_____

_____

_____

_____

_____

_____

_____

Chapter 10
Short, Light-skin, and Cute

When we start dating, there is an expectation that men have to be on point and near perfect. I have a problem with this theory. Now, don't kill me, sis... Just hear me out. Men are human beings just like we are. They make mistakes, and they don't know everything - even though they like to pretend that they do. Society has created this image that men must be perfect. They have to meet this standard that is somewhat unattainable. I noticed that when I started dating my fiancé, everyone was telling me to leave him alone because he wasn't ready to be in a relationship. They would say, "He ain't ish, girl." Now, let's rewind to a couple years prior when I was going through a rough patch and not mentally ready for a relationship. Those same women were telling me that a man should be patient with me. Wait a minute?! Do you see the double standard? When a woman isn't ready, a man should wait for her. However, when the shoe is on the other foot, it's "Girl leave him alone." How unfair is this? This is when I realized that society places unfair standards on women and men when it comes to relationships. (Well, in general, but that's another book.)

This whole situation really began to take its toll on me until I made the decision that I was okay in my situation for that time. Truth be told, I thought he was worth the wait. Yes, I said it. Hear me out... I'm not saying to just get into something with a guy and just wait. I'm saying that if you find a good man, and he has good intentions for you, it is okay to give him the time that he needs to be ready to make a lifelong commitment to you. Now remember, I sought God in my situation, so I'm not telling you to do this on your own. I just want you to understand that you can't let society or what your friend says dictate your relationship. They both will have you out here single and alone, fighting for something that doesn't even benefit your life.

Let me get a little more detailed about this topic because I'm sure most of you are already done with me. Thank Goodness, you've already read most of the book. So, listen up! I'm not saying to just go out there and pick up random unqualified men. That is the last thing I want you to do, but I want you to understand that men are not perfect. They don't have it all together like the story book says. They are trying to figure this thing called life out just like us. I see so many of my female friends cutting guys off because he has made a mistake or two, but so have you. If this man is showing progress, he listens to you, he cares about you, and he takes the time to include you in his life, it is ok give him a break. I understand that you were hurt five years ago, but how are you ever going to allow your husband to find you if you don't let go of the past?

I find that most of us are just out here fighting. We fight with our boss, with other women, and with the men who we attempt to date. We fight for respect, and we fight for our rights. Sometimes, I believe that we have gotten so accustomed to fighting that we don't even know how to just be in peace. We have to choose our battles wisely. We are so afraid of being hurt and disappointed again that we fight to preserve ourselves. It may sound scary, but we have to let our guards down to experience love. Love is a risk, but that's why you have the guidance of the Holy Spirit to grant you discernment to allow the right people into your life.

Yes, I understand that some men are just full of mess and aren't worth the time. I get that they exist. Still, I wonder how many times you have moved on from a man who wasn't like your father. "My dad doesn't treat me that way." Well, I guarantee that if you talk to your mom, she would tell you that you father was not perfect in his twenties either. You're comparing a fifty or sixty-year-old man to a young man who is still growing and learning. I'm not saying not to have standards, but understand that a lot of our men, especially black men, don't know how to be emotional and how to express themselves. Our men are being attacked daily. Once they go out that door, the world is on their backs. A wise woman told me a long time, "You have to be his peace. His world can be falling apart, but he has to trust that when he comes home, there is peace." I wonder how many of our good men are going home where he is constantly at war with his woman.

I titled this chapter: "Short, Light-Skin, and Cute" because I really wanted you all to understand that not only are men imperfect, but neither are they all tall, dark, and handsome. Society has just completely jacked us up with the expectations of our men. We can't all get the tall, dark, and handsome guy, because it just leaves room for so many good men of different physical characteristics to get away. I have news for you sis, the "one" is probably not going to look anything like you typically date, but that's the beauty of it. Personally, when I stopped dating what I considered my type, things began to work for me. The one that you least expect will be the one who changes your world.

Don't let a good man who may be a little imperfect and short get away because you're comparing him to the man that your friend or your favorite celebrity has. God knows what type of man you need. Most importantly, He knows who will to be the best teammate for you. You two will have to work together, raise children together, have each another's back, and above all, love one another. God knows who that man is, so please don't pass him up because he doesn't do something that society says he should or because he's older than you prefer.

When I met my fiancé and learned that he is four years younger than I am, I had no intentions of getting serious with him. A long time ago, somewhere between dating and being single, I promised myself that I would never date a younger man. Oh, the irony! I know that God has a sense of humor, because I tried with all my being not to develop feelings for him. I just thought we would have a fling because not only was he younger, but he was also my neighbor. I know! I know! Never date the neighbor. Yeah, well. I did it. There I was just breaking all the rules for this guy, right? As it was happening, I just didn't care.

Those things were insignificant compared to how much he loved Christ, how he treated me, and how he was just a good person. He was honest. When he said he was going to do something, he did it. When he was wrong, he apologized. He treated his mother and sister like a queen and a princess. Most importantly, he always progressed. We were far from perfect when we first started dating, but there was always something special there. His age or where he lived didn't mean a thing when it came to how he treated me. I thought he was worth the risk, so I made an executive decision to break the rules. When you meet *the one*, you will probably feel the same way.

Scriptures on Loving Unconditionally

- ♥ 1 Corinthians 13:4-7 – "Love is patient and kind; love does not envy or boast; it is not arrogant or rude. It does not insist on its own way; it is not irritable or resentful; it does not rejoice at wrongdoing, but rejoices with the truth. Love bears all things, believes all things, hopes all things, endures all things."

- ♥ 1 John 4:18 – "There is no fear in love, but perfect love casts out fear. For fear has to do with punishment, and whoever fears has not been perfected in love."

- ♥ 1 John 3:20 – "For whenever our heart condemns us, God is greater than our heart, and he knows everything."

- ♥ Romans 2:1 – "Therefore you have no excuse, O man, every one of you who judges. For in passing judgment on another you condemn yourself, because you, the judge, practice the very same things."

- ♥ Ephesians 5:1 – "Therefore be imitators of God, as beloved children."

- ♥ John 15:13 – "Greater love has no one than this, that someone lay down His life for His friends."
- ♥ John 15:12 – "This is my commandment, that you love one another as I have loved you."
- ♥ John 3:16 - "For God so loved the world, that He gave His only Son, that whoever believes in Him should not perish but have eternal life."
- ♥ Romans 3:23 – "For all have sinned and fall short of the glory of God."
- ♥ Ephesians 5:25 – "Husbands, love your wives, as Christ loved the church and gave himself up for her."
- ♥ Romans 5:8 – "But God shows his love for us in that while we were still sinners, Christ died for us."
- ♥ 1 John 3:17 – "But if anyone has the world's goods and sees his brother in need, yet closes his heart against him, how does God's love abide in him?"
- ♥ 1 Corinthians 16:14 – "Let all that you do be done in love."

Notes

Notes

_____
_____
_____
_____
_____
_____
_____
_____
_____
_____
_____
_____
_____
_____
_____
_____
_____
_____
_____
_____
_____
_____

Chapter 11
Friendship Before the Bedroom

When women think of being in love, we equate that to passion and romantic gestures. On the contrary, love is far more than just romance and lovemaking. There is this false idea that if you lack any of these things, you are not loved. However, that is far from the truth. We tend to worship this image of what we think a relationship should be. When the relationship isn't filled with passion and excitement, we feel as though the man does not love us. Many times, women not only jump in and out of relationships, but some jump in and out of bed with the men they are considering being in a relationship with. I'm not saying that all women are promiscuous, but what I am saying is that we don't allow ourselves the time to really get to know these men before becoming intimate with them.

Intimacy is such a beautiful thing, but God created an order of how we should develop intimacy based on His word not ours. Society says that you should "test drive the car before you buy it" or, in other words, that you should have sex to keep a man. We've made having sex such a trivial thing that it is starting to damage us. If we really understood how truly intimate sex is, then I don't think that we would do it as often or with as many people. Your body is so precious that God intended for us to only share it with one person. When we allow a man to enter inside of us, we ingest of all his emotions. Likewise, if we sleep with multiple men, we are carrying the cares of all those men. Do you know how serious and damaging that can be to a woman? As women, we are already emotional beings. Therefore, we must be careful with who we decide to share those emotions with - let alone our bodies. No matter how strong we claim to be, we cannot separate our emotions from sex and all that ties that comes along with it.

When you open yourself up to multiple people, it places you in a position to be hurt, and your heart becomes hardened. God never intended for us, as women to be hard. I think when Steve Harvey said that we need to act like a lady and think like a man, we misunderstood his point. I think he wanted us to understand the *way* a man thinks, not to physically think like him. In fact, that's impossible for a woman, because God did not build us that way. As we previously discussed, when we enter seasons before they are ready to be harvested, we create issues for ourselves. Simply put, as single women, we should not be having sex with a man who is not our husband. When we have pre-marital sex, it opens the door for sexually transmitted diseases, pregnancy out of wedlock, and the most damaging of all, emotional scarring. These are all things that God never intended for us.

It's time for women to take the power that we hold and use it to gain the maximum benefit out of life and relationships. Imagine if we began to focus on friendship first, allowing love to develop based on who we are without sex ever being involved. Could you imagine how many more successful relationships would exist? Many of those guys that seem to be so appealing wouldn't even make the cut. That's because sex clouds judgement. We wouldn't have to deal with the regret of being intimate with someone who we realize by month four was a complete jerk and not worth our time. Our bodies are precious, and we must begin to treat it as such.

I had a friend tell me a long time ago that we have titles – friend, girlfriend, fiancée, or wife - for a reason. The problem is that when we are a friend, we are acting as girlfriend and taking on those tasks. Then, when we are a girlfriend, we are acting as a wife, and it's time to stop crossing those lines. We are spending too much time in the gray area when it should be black and white. We spend years in "situationships" because we have taken permanent residency in the gray area. Why would a man marry a woman who he is already acting as his wife? Don't get me wrong there are some men out there who are just good guys. Those good guys will marry you because they love you. Yet, most men will stay in the gray area if you let them. It's comfortable, and it's easy.

Make up your mind about what you want and stick to that. You deserve to be loved the way that God intended for you to be loved. I am not here to pass judgment on anyone reading this who has participated in premarital sex, because I am not a virgin nor am I married. I discovered that sex was something that I struggled with as a young woman. It was how I expressed my love. However, when I sought God and His love, He showed me that I didn't need sex to find true love. Sex is just icing on a cake. You don't really need icing to enjoy the cake, but you do need a good cake to enjoy the dessert. There are necessary steps (building a foundation) that go into making a good cake in addition to the ingredients (characteristics). Without those, you just end up with a flat nasty cake. I wonder how many of you are eating a nasty cake with good icing. It's not very tasty, is it?

My point is that sex is not necessary in finding the love your heart desires.
When you truly love someone, the sex will be amazing. God already has His hand in that. God is involved in more than just your physical. When you become intimate with your husband, it will be physical, spiritual, emotional, and mental. The

world says that you need sex to please a man, but a real man will fall in love with your mind and your spirit. Don't believe what Satan suggests when he tells you that sex is a necessity, because it's not. Take the time to get to know the man you are dealing with. Learn to be his friend before you make the decision to become intimate with him. Moreover, believe that there is a man out there who will love you and be willing to wait until you are married to have sex with you. I never thought that day would come for me, but it is here and I am living it. The same thing can happen for you.

Scriptures on Premarital Sex

- ♥ Hebrews 13:4 – "Let marriage be held in honor among all, and let the marriage bed be undefiled, for God will judge the sexually immoral and adulterous."
- ♥ 1 Thessalonians 4:3-5 – "For this is the will of God, your sanctification: that you abstain from sexual immorality; that each one of you know how to control his own body in holiness and honor, not in the passion of lust like the Gentiles who do not know God."
- ♥ 1 Corinthians 6:18-20 – "Flee from sexual immorality. Every other sin a person commits is outside the body, but the sexually immoral person sins against his own body. Or do you not know that your body is a temple of the Holy Spirit within you, whom you have from God? You are not your own, for you were bought with a price. So glorify God in your body."
- ♥ 1 Corinthians 7:2 – "But because of the temptation to sexual immorality, each man should have his own wife and each woman her own husband."

- ♥ 1 Corinthians 6:9-10 – "Or do you not know that the unrighteous will not inherit the kingdom of God? Do not be deceived: neither the sexually immoral, nor idolaters, nor adulterers, nor men who practice homosexuality, nor thieves, nor the greedy, nor drunkards, nor revilers, nor swindlers will inherit the kingdom of God."
- ♥ Galatians 5:19 – "Now the works of the flesh are evident: sexual immorality, impurity, sensuality."
- ♥ 1 Corinthians 7:8-9 – "To the unmarried and the widows I say that it is good for them to remain single as I am. But if they cannot exercise self-control, they should marry. For it is better to marry than to burn with passion."
- ♥ 1 Corinthians 10:1 – "No temptation has overtaken you that is not common to man. God is faithful, and he will not let you be tempted beyond your ability, but with the temptation he will also provide the way of escape, that you may be able to endure it."

♥ Galatians 5:19 – "Now the works of the flesh are evident: sexual immorality, impurity, sensuality.

Notes

Notes

_____
_____
_____
_____
_____
_____
_____
_____
_____
_____
_____
_____
_____
_____
_____
_____
_____
_____
_____
_____
_____
_____
_____
_____

Chapter 12
Your Best Days Are Ahead

Oh, my goodness! I can't believe we are here! Now that you have a good understanding of what it takes to find that love that you have so long desired, it's time to declare and decree that the best days are ahead of you. You must begin to believe this with every part of your being. You have to rid yourself of worry, doubt, and fear. You know what you need most, self-love. When you believe that you are worth true love, you will receive true love. God truly wants the best for you. If you never receive anything from this book, remember to keep your eyes focused on Jesus. No matter what! He loves you so much. The Bible says, "Take delight in the Lord and he will give you the desires of your heart." Enjoy Him, sis. Spend time with Him. Read His word. Get to know who He is, not what religion says He is. He wants you to enjoy heaven on heart, and that includes receiving ALL the desires of your heart.

I believe that if you really begin to take hold of your true identity then you have the authority to have the life you want. I encourage you to change your mindset. If you are taking the time to understand and know God then you will learn all about His promises but you have to read His word. Wake up every morning and begin to confess the things that you are praying for over your life. (See page 107) You CAN do ALL things through Christ but you must believe that first so your life is in your hands. Your thoughts will determine where you go. If you have negative thoughts, then it's time to change what you hear and what you see. What are you watching? Who are you listening to? What contributes to these thoughts? It's time to remove whatever those factors are and take control of your life. Take the limits off. The sky is the limit and it's time to explore.

So here we are sis, the end of the book and I pray that these pages have been beneficial to your journey. I hope that this book will allow you to take charge and bring you to a place where you truly understand that you have the love and the life that you have yearned for. I want you to know that this book was written just for you. God placed this on my heart because he knew you were going to read it. This is not just a coincidence. I want every single woman who reads this book to know how it feels to be a wife. Although I have shared a lot throughout this book I would like to share my testimony with you...

I started writing this book in July of 2015. As I stated before, God revealed to me what I was (and so many women were) doing wrong in our relationships and how we needed to just focus on Him. He held the mirror up and exposed a lot of my faults and the things that I was doing wrong. As I began to make the adjustments, I promised myself that God would be the first thing I thought of in the morning and the last thing I thought about at night. At one point, I was so focused on my boyfriend that in so many ways, he became my God. But, God wasn't going to honor me while I was putting someone else before Him.

When I realized that, I began to put more trust in God than I had ever done before. I started loving on myself more than ever because I really understood His love. I began to make confessions every night based on God's word over my life and relationship. I began to understand that for my relationship to work, I had to honor God first, and that included with my body. I also began to understand that my boyfriend was an imperfect human being, and I made the decision to love him regardless. I honored each season based on God's plan even though I did not always understand it. I continued to acknowledge Him, and He continued to direct my paths. There were times where I was afraid. There were times when I feared my ability to write a book without any type of psychology degree or certification. God continued to assure me that I didn't need to be qualified by anyone but Him. This message was hand wrapped and gifted to me from Him for women who were having the same issues that I had experienced. He has confirmed multiple times that in order to reap the benefits of His love, we must change our mindset and that is exactly what I did.

On April 9, 2017, my boyfriend asked me to be his wife, and we are now planning our wedding. We are planning to get married in July of 2018 in Cancun, Mexico. Our relationship wouldn't be what it is today if I hadn't given it to

God. I truly believe that every woman should experience the joy that occurs when the man she loves asks them to be his wife. I hope that this book will help you to understand your position in Christ and how worthy you are to thrive in a loving, healthy relationship. You are the righteousness of God. He wants the best for your life. Allow Him to have His way, and I promise you will also have a testimony. I am always here to pray and talk to anyone who needs an ear. I pray that this book was a blessing to you. God bless!

Before I leave you... there is one more thing. If you do not know Christ as your Lord and Savior, I pray that you will invite him into your life and heart by saying the prayer of salvation. Once you have said the prayer, find a bible based church to get a good understanding of the Bible. Start to spend time reading your Bible every day in order to renew your mind from old habits and behaviors. I promise you will never be the same again. Say this simple prayer out loud:

"Heavenly Father, I acknowledge that Jesus is Lord. I believe that Jesus died for my sins and rose from the dead. I repent of my sins. Come into my heart and be the Lord of my life. I am cleansed of my past. Fill me with your spirit, Lord."

Daily Affirmations

- ♥ I am worth every blessing that life has to offer.
- ♥ Christ is in me.
- ♥ I trust God with everything. He is my source.
- ♥ I am whole. Nothing missing. Nothing broken.
- ♥ I am the righteousness of God
- ♥ My best days are ahead of me.
- ♥ God has a specific plan just for me.
- ♥ I am beautiful. I am successful. I am intelligent.
- ♥ I am worthy of a loving relationship.
- ♥ This is the day that the Lord has made. I will rejoice and be glad in it.
- ♥ I attract relationships, situations, and opportunities that work for my good.

- ♥ I attract only positive and encouraging people to my life.
- ♥ This is going to be the best day of my life.
- ♥ I am a giver. I give effortlessly and frequently.
- ♥ I deserve the best in life.
- ♥ I look at the good in every situation.
- ♥ My relationship is centered and focused on God.
- ♥ I am out of debt.
- ♥ I am intelligent and I make the best decisions for my life.
- ♥ I am in a relationship that is healthy and focused on God.
- ♥ I have the wisdom of Christ.
- ♥ I deserve to be love and be in a healthy fulfilling relationship.
- ♥ I am confident. I am not insecure or jealous of any other woman.

- ♥ I am fearless.
- ♥ I follow my dreams.
- ♥ Money comes to me effortlessly and frequently.
- ♥ I am blessed and highly favored.
- ♥ I am a/an _____ (fill in career). I love make money doing what I love.
- ♥ I have a fulfilling and successful career.
- ♥ I will live my best life.
- ♥ I am beautiful. I love my body.
- ♥ I walk in love always.
- ♥ I am whole, nothing missing, nothing broken.
- ♥ My body healthy, healed and fully functioning the way God intended.
- ♥ I am not petty. I am powerful.

I challenge you to write down the things that you are praying for and find a scripture related to it. Find out what His word says about what you are believing Him for, and say those confessions every day. I guarantee you will see manifestation in your life. I have created this area just for your confessions. Trust Him & enjoy!

Notes

_____
_____
_____
_____
_____
_____
_____
_____
_____
_____
_____
_____
_____
_____
_____
_____
_____
_____
_____
_____
_____
_____
_____
_____

Notes

_____

_____

_____

_____

_____

_____

_____

_____

_____

_____

_____

_____

_____

_____

_____

_____

_____

_____

_____

_____

_____

_____

_____

_____

Notes

_____
_____
_____
_____
_____
_____
_____
_____
_____
_____
_____
_____
_____
_____
_____
_____
_____
_____
_____
_____
_____
_____
_____

Notes

Notes

Notes

Notes

_____

_____

_____

_____

_____

_____

_____

_____

_____

_____

_____

_____

_____

_____

_____

_____

_____

_____

_____

_____

_____

_____

_____

_____

Notes

Notes

_____

_____

_____

_____

_____

_____

_____

_____

_____

_____

_____

_____

_____

_____

_____

_____

_____

_____

_____

_____

_____

_____

_____

Notes